W9-DHI-266

Up Close and GROSS

Microscopic Creatures

GROSS BODY INVADERS

by Ruth Owen

Consultant: Suzy Gazlay, M.A.
Recipient, Presidential Award
for Excellence in Science Teaching

BEARPORT
PUBLISHING

New York, New York

Credits

Cover and title page, © Clouds Hill Imaging/www.lastrefuge.co.uk; 3, © Robert Harding Picture Library/Superstock; 4, © Eye of Science/Science Photo Library; 5, © Eye of Science/Science Photo Library; 6, © Eye of Science/Science Photo Library; 7, © Clouds Hill Imaging/www.lastrefuge.co.uk; 8, © Eye of Science/Science Photo Library; 9, © Steve Gschmeissner/Science Photo Library; 10, © Courtesy of Syngenta; 11, © Robert Harding Picture Library/Superstock; 12, © Kenneth H. Thomas/Science Photo Library; 13, © Clouds Hill Imaging/www.lastrefuge.co.uk; 14, © Zdorov Kirill Vladimirovich/Shutterstock; 15T, © Dr. Tony Brain/Science Photo Library; 15B, © CNRI/Science Photo Library; 16, © Dr. P. Marazzi/Science Photo Library; 17, © David Scharf/Science Photo Library; 18, © Eric Grave/Science Photo Library; 19, © Ron Boardman, Life Science Images/Science Photo Library; 20, © Shutterstock; 21, © Mikhail Melnikov/Shutterstock; 22T, © Pascal Goetgheluck/Science Photo Library; 22C, © Scott Bauer/US Department of Agriculture/Science Photo Library; 22B, © David Scharf/Science Photo Library.

Publisher: Kenn Goin
Senior Editor: Lisa Wiseman
Creative Director: Spencer Brinker
Design: Alix Wood
Photo Researcher: Ruby Tuesday Books Ltd

Library of Congress Cataloging-in-Publication Data

Owen, Ruth.
  Gross body invaders / by Ruth Owen.
    p. cm. — (Up close and gross: microscopic creatures)
  Includes bibliographical references and index.
  ISBN-13: 978-1-61772-127-4 (library binding)
  ISBN-10: 1-61772-127-1 (library binding)
  1. Parasites—Juvenile literature. I. Title.
  QR251.O94 2011
  578.6'5—dc22

                              2010044416

Published in the United States of America by Bearport Publishing Company, Inc.

For more information, write to Bearport Publishing Company, Inc., 101 Fifth Avenue, Suite 6R, New York, New York 10003. Printed in the United States of America in North Mankato, Minnesota.

122010
10810CGD

10 9 8 7 6 5 4 3 2 1

Contents

Who's Living on and in Your Body?

When people think about where animals live, they might think of a forest or the ocean. They probably don't think of their own bodies as a home for living things—but they should. The human body provides food and a place to stay and **reproduce** for millions of body invaders!

Some body invaders, such as fleas, are big enough to see using just your eyes. Others, such as **bacteria**, are so small that you need to use a **microscope** to see them.

In this book you will have a chance to see amazing images of some body invaders. Using powerful microscopes, scientists have zoomed in on these living things to show them up close and in great detail. So get ready to be grossed out by the creatures living on and inside of YOU!

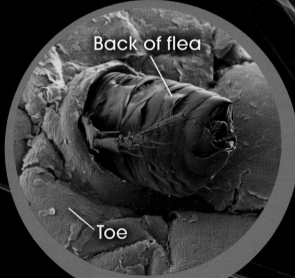

Back of flea

Toe

This tiny body invader, a chigoe flea, has burrowed itself into the skin between a person's toes. It is drinking the person's blood!

Thousands of different types of bacteria live on and inside the human body. Some types of bacteria are harmful, causing illness and disease. Others do important jobs, such as breaking down food in the stomach.

These bacteria are shown **3,400 TIMES** their actual size!

Bacteria that cause bad breath

This is a human tongue as seen under a microscope. The yellow strands are the bacteria that cause bad breath.

Itchy, Scratchy Head Lice

Head lice are insects that live in human hair. They feed by drinking blood from the heads of their victims.

Soon after invading a person's head, a female head louse will begin laying up to eight eggs, or nits, a day. She sticks each egg onto a piece of hair using glue that she makes inside her body. After about seven days the eggs hatch into young lice, called **nymphs**. It takes the nymphs just two weeks to become adult lice and begin laying their own eggs. This means that hundreds of lice can be living on a person's head in just a few weeks!

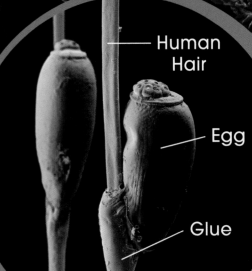

Human Hair

Egg

Glue

Head lice eggs are smaller than a pinhead.

Head lice cannot jump, but they can walk from the hair of one person to another if two people's heads touch. They can also spread from one person to another on items such as combs, pillows, or hats. Head lice make the victim's head feel very itchy!

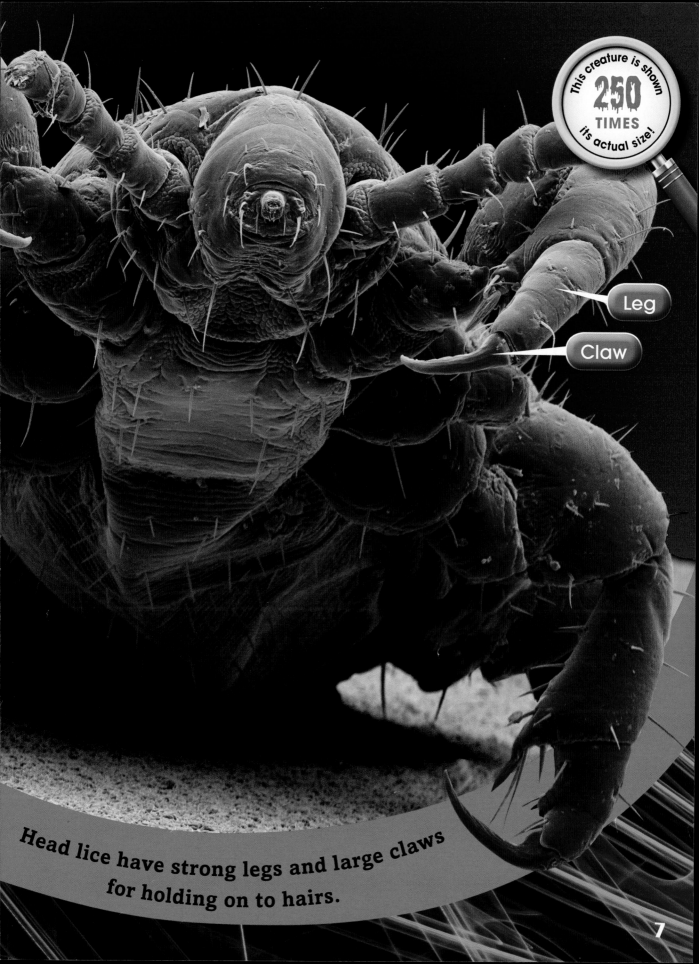

This creature is shown **250** TIMES its actual size!

Leg

Claw

Head lice have strong legs and large claws for holding on to hairs.

Face-Invading Eyelash Mites

Humans have lots of small hairs growing on their faces. Eyebrows, eyelashes, nose hair, and lip hair, known as a mustache, all grow out of tiny openings in the skin called **follicles**. The eyelash mite is a microscopic body invader that can live in all these hair follicles on human faces.

The worm-like eyelash mite lives head-down in the follicle. Here it feeds on skin oils and pieces of dead skin. The mite doesn't hurt humans, but if too many mites try to live in one follicle, the piece of hair could fall out.

The eyelash mite is so good at digesting its food that the creature doesn't produce any waste such as **urine** or poop. That's good news for humans because it means people don't have eyelash mite waste on their faces!

An eyelash mite that has been magnified

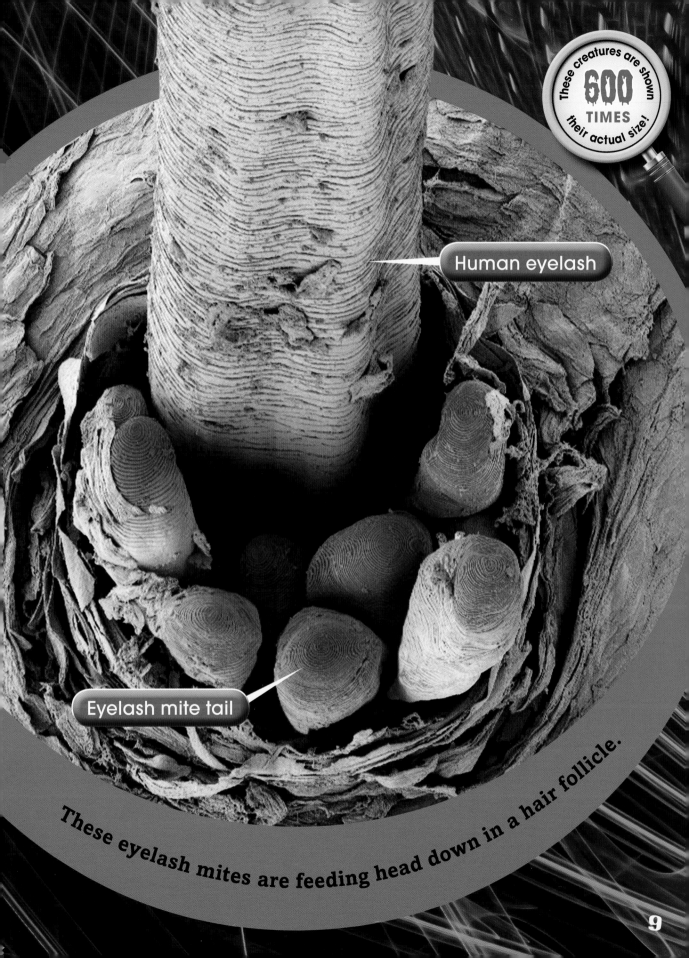

These creatures are shown **600** TIMES their actual size!

Human eyelash

Eyelash mite tail

These eyelash mites are feeding head down in a hair follicle.

Deadly Mosquito Bites

Adult mosquitoes feed on fruit and **nectar** from plants. In order to produce eggs, however, a female mosquito must get **nourishment** by sucking the blood of a human or some other **mammal**. Most types of mosquitoes are not dangerous to people, but some kinds of Anopheles (AH-no-fee-liz) mosquitoes can transmit the disease **malaria** to humans.

Malaria is caused by tiny living things called **parasites**. When a mosquito that is carrying the malaria parasites bites a human, it passes the parasites from its body to the body of its victim. The parasites then invade the person's blood and liver, causing great damage. More than one million people worldwide die from malaria each year.

Mosquito net

People who live where malaria is a threat sometimes protect themselves from getting the disease by sleeping under nets treated with chemicals that kill mosquitoes.

About 90 percent of malaria deaths happen in Africa. People are also at risk in parts of Asia and Central and South America. Malaria medicines are available, and it's important that infected people get treatment fast, before the disease becomes life threatening.

This creature is shown **100 TIMES** its actual size!

Mouthparts

A mosquito uses a long, jagged mouthpart to pierce its victim's skin.

Bloodsucking Black-Legged Ticks

Black-legged **ticks** live in the Northeast, Midwest, Southeast, and Western United States. Adult ticks feed by sucking blood from mammals, including humans! These ticks are sometimes called deer ticks because they often feed on deer.

The black-legged tick lives on plants or in long grass. When a person passes by, a tick can climb onto the person's clothing and crawl to a warm, dark place on the person's body, such as an armpit. It then pierces its victim's skin with its mouthparts and starts to suck blood. If it is not discovered, the tick will continue feeding for several days until it is a balloon-like, blood-filled blob!

A blood-filled tick inside a dog's ear

Black-legged ticks carry the bacteria that cause Lyme disease. People infected with Lyme disease may feel as if they have the flu. In serious cases, people may suffer damage to their hearts or **nervous systems**.

This black-legged tick has its mouthparts buried in a hamster's skin.

13

Rat Fleas and the Bubonic Plague

Blood-sucking fleas do not just bite animals, such as dogs and rats. If there are no animals nearby to get blood from, fleas may bite humans. This can sometimes be very dangerous to the victims.

In the **Middle Ages**, the deadly **bubonic plague** was spread across Europe by a type of flea called an Oriental rat flea. Back then, most towns and villages were dirty places. Many rats and fleas lived alongside humans. Some of the rats carried the bacteria that cause bubonic plague. When fleas sucked blood from the infected rats, they picked up the bacteria. Then if the fleas bit a human they passed the bacteria to them, spreading plague. At the time, millions of people were killed by the disease!

Oriental rat fleas can still carry bubonic plague today. Thankfully, most people no longer share their homes with rats and fleas, so the disease is rarely spread to humans. Rodents such as prairie dogs can carry rat fleas, however. People should avoid handling these animals.

An Oriental rat flea clinging to the fur of a rat

These bubonic plague bacteria have been magnified so that they look 2,400 times bigger than they actually are!

The Horror of Hookworms

Some kinds of adult hookworms can live in the human **digestive system**. There, a female hookworm will produce thousands of eggs during her lifetime. The eggs leave the body in a person's poop and can end up on the ground.

Young worms called **larvae** hatch from the eggs and live on the ground until they come into contact with a human victim. They burrow through the person's skin and are carried in the blood to the lungs. They are then coughed up into the mouth and swallowed. Once the larvae are swallowed, they end up attached to the **small intestine**. Here, they become adults and begin feeding on the victim's blood.

Many poor countries do not have clean ways of getting rid of human waste, so poop containing hookworm eggs can end up on the ground. When larvae hatch from the eggs, people may come into contact with them, either on their hands or bare feet.

Hookworm larvae

This hookworm larvae is burrowing into a person's foot.

Tooth-like structure

A hookworm attaches to its victim's small intestine using tooth-like structures.

Terrible Tapeworms

Tapeworms are parasites that live in human digestive systems. They feed by taking nutrients from their victims' bodies. When this occurs, the victims may lose weight.

One way that humans can become infected with tapeworms is by eating raw or undercooked pork or beef that has already been infected with tapeworm larvae, or young. So how do the tapeworm larvae get into the meat? Poop that contains tapeworm eggs from infected humans can end up in places where pigs and cattle eat or drink. Once inside the animals, the eggs hatch. The tapeworm larvae that come out grow and spread to the animals' muscles, or meat. If people eat this infected meat without cooking it properly, the larvae will still be alive. Once the meat is eaten, the larvae will end up in the victims' intestines. There they will grow into adult tapeworms.

Tapeworms have flat, ribbon-like bodies. Some types can grow to be 30 feet (9 m) long!

This tapeworm was taken from inside a human digestive system.

Hooks

Sucker

A tapeworm attaches itself to the wall of a victim's intestines using hooks and suckers.

Hungry Horseflies

Female horseflies need a meal of blood to help their eggs develop. They get blood from biting humans and other large mammals, such as horses and cattle. A bite from this body invader feels like a hot needle piercing the skin!

To get its blood, a horsefly lands on its victim and attacks! It has two saw-like body parts called mandibles. It uses the mandibles to cut a hole in the victim's skin. When the blood starts flowing from the wound, the fly licks it up. A horsefly attack isn't dangerous to a human, but the bites can be painful and itchy.

Horseflies are sneaky and often attack people on the back of their legs or necks. Scientists don't know how the flies choose where to bite, but they seem to pick spots where they won't be seen. By the time the victim realizes the fly is there, it's too late!

A horsefly sucking blood from a person's hand

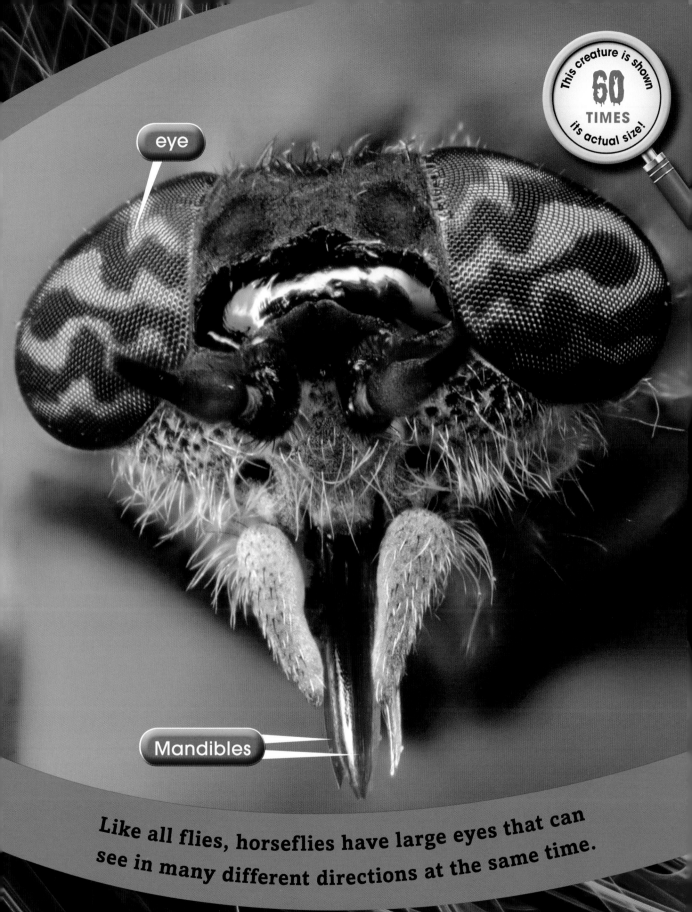

eye

This creature is shown **60** TIMES its actual size!

Mandibles

Like all flies, horseflies have large eyes that can see in many different directions at the same time.

Getting Up Close

The amazing close-up photographs in this book were created using a very powerful microscope. It is called a scanning **electron** microscope, or SEM.

Microscopes make things look bigger. A scanning electron microscope can show what things look like hundreds of times their real size.

How were the photos in this book created?

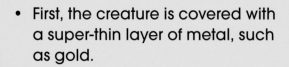

- First, the creature is covered with a super-thin layer of metal, such as gold.

- Next, the SEM passes a beam of tiny particles called electrons over the creature. The electrons bounce off the metal around the creature and create electrical signals. These signals are turned into a black-and-white image of the creature on a computer.

- Scientists then add color to the SEM image using a computer.

Glossary

bacteria (bak-TIHR-ee-uh) tiny life forms that can be seen only under a microscope; some bacteria can cause disease, but some are helpful in keeping humans and animals healthy

bubonic plague (byoo-BON-ik PLAYG) a deadly disease that is spread by fleas and rodents such as rats

digestive system (dye-JESS-tiv SISS-tuhm) the group of organs in people or animals that helps break down food so the body can use it for fuel

electron (i-LEK-tron) a tiny particle that is found in atoms, the building blocks of all matter; electrons carry electrical charges

follicles (FOL-i-kuhlz) tiny openings, or pores, in the skin that hairs grow from

larvae (LAR-vee) the worm-like form of many kinds of young insects; the singular form is *larva*

malaria (muh-LAIR-ee-uh) a disease, transmitted to humans by the bite of an infected female Anopheles mosquito, which causes chills, fever, sweating, and even death

mammal (MAM-uhl) an animal that is warm-blooded, nurses its young with milk, and has hair or fur on its skin

microscope (MYE-kruh-skohp) a tool used to see things that are too small to see with the eyes alone

Middle Ages (MID-uhl AJE-iz) a time period in European history from about 500 AD to around 1500

nectar (NEK-tur) a sweet liquid produced by plants

nervous systems (NUR-vuhss SISS-tuhmz) systems in the bodies of humans and animals that carry instructions from the brain to the rest of the body; the nervous system is made up of the brain, spinal cord, and nerves

nourishment (NUR-ish-muhnt) something needed by a living thing in order for it to live and grow

nymphs (NIMFS) the young of some types of insects

parasites (PA-ruh-*sites*) living things that get food by living on or in another living thing

reproduce (*ree*-pruh-DOOSS) to produce more of a living thing

small intestine (SMAWL in-TESS-tin) a long, narrow tube in the digestive system where nutrients from food are passed into the blood

ticks (TIKS) tiny animals with eight legs; ticks are not insects but are arachnids, a group that includes spiders and mites

urine (YOOR-uhn) liquid waste produced by people or animals

Index

Bibliography

Centers for Disease Control and Prevention: *www.cdc.gov*

Institute of Food and Agricultural Sciences, University of Florida: *edis.ifas.ufl.edu/ig087*

The World Health Organization: *www.who.int/en/*

Read More

Davies, Nicola. *What's Eating You?: Parasites—The Inside Story.* Somerville, MA: Candlewick Press (2009).

Tilden, Thomasine E. Lewis. *Belly-Busting Worm Invasions!: Parasites That Love Your Insides! (24/7: Science Behind the Scenes).* New York: Scholastic (2008).

Twist, Clint. *Fleas (Nature's Minibeasts).* New York: Gareth Stevens (2005).

Learn More Online

To learn more about body invaders, visit
www.bearportpublishing.com/UpCloseandGross

About The Author

Ruth Owen has been writing children's books for more than ten years. She lives in Cornwall, England, just minutes from the ocean. Ruth loves gardening and caring for her family of llamas.